D1541278

The Progressive Movement 1900–1920
Efforts to Reform America's New Industrial Society ™

PROGRESSIVE LEADERS

The Platforms and Policies of America's Reform Politicians

Lois Sakany

rosen central
Primary Source™

The Rosen Publishing Group, Inc., New York

Published in 2006 by The Rosen Publishing Group, Inc.
29 East 21st Street, New York, NY 10010

Library of Congress Cataloging-in-Publication Data

Sakany, Lois.
Progressive leaders: the platforms and policies of America's reform politicians/by Lois Sakany.— 1st ed.
        p. cm.—(The progressive movement, 1900–1920: efforts to reform America's new industrial society)
Includes bibliographical references and index.
ISBN 1-4042-0193-9 (lib. bdg.)
ISBN 1-4042-0855-0 (pbk. bdg.)
6-pack ISBN 1-4042-6192-3
1. United States—Politics and government—1901–1953—Juvenile literature. 2. Politicians—United States—History—20th century—Juvenile literature. 3. Progressivism (United States politics)—Juvenile literature. 4. Social problems—United States—History—20th century—Juvenile literature. 5. United States—Social conditions—1865–1918—Juvenile literature. I. Title. II. Series: Progressive movement, 1900–1920.
E743.S24 2005
324.2732'7—dc22

                                                                    2004002682

Manufactured in the United States of America

On the cover: Top: Robert M. La Follette in 1924 addressing voters in Washington, D.C. Bottom: Two workers without safety equipment pour molten metal at the International Harvester's Milwaukee Works, 1902.

Photo credits: Cover (top) Culver Pictures; cover (bottom) pp. 7, 8 Wisconsin Historical Society; pp. 5, 23, 25 Library of Congress Prints and Photographs Division; p. 10 © Corbis; p. 12 © Snark/Art Resource, NY; p. 13 General Research Division, The New York Public Library, Astor, Lenox and Tilden Foundations; pp. 15, 17, 21 © Bettmann/Corbis; p. 20 © Hulton/Archive/Getty Images; p. 27 Ohio Historical Society

Designer: Les Kanturek; Editor: Joann Jovinelly; Photo Researcher: Amy Feinberg

Contents

Chapter One

The Changing of the Guard

During the late 1800s, the United States experienced a period of rapid development. Its population soared as immigrants arrived by the thousands from Europe and Asia. Fewer people lived and worked in rural America. More people moved to urban areas like New York City and Chicago to work in factories.

From 1870 to 1900, there were three economic depressions. Farmers suffered the most during these downtimes. They demanded change. Their leaders, whether Democratic or Republican, did little to help them. To help solve their problems, farmers formed the Populist Party to push their ideas forward.

By 1896, the Populist Party had collapsed from lack of support. However, it influenced the thinking of many Democratic and Republican leaders. The new ideas of Populism combined with the more conservative ideas of the

William Jennings Bryan (1860–1925) is seen in this 1896 photograph as a Democratic presidential nominee. Bryan, a Progressive politician and gifted public speaker, ran unsuccessfully for the U.S. presidency in 1896, 1900, and 1908. This political cartoon from 1900, the same year that Bryan ran as the Populist presidential nominee, features his head on a python swallowing the Democratic Party donkey.

Democrats and Republicans signaled the start of the Progressive movement.

One of the first leaders of this period was William Jennings Bryan. Born in Salem, Illinois, in 1860, Bryan graduated from the Union College of Law in Chicago in 1883. In 1887, Bryan moved to Lincoln, Nebraska. He was elected to Congress as a Democrat, but his support came mostly from Populists. He was called the "Great Commoner" because he stood up for ordinary Americans.

Bryan ran for president three times as the Democratic nominee. For his 1896 presidential campaign, he pushed for the "free silver" policy. After the Civil War, Republicans started a policy to make sure that every dollar was backed by gold. During tough times, borrowers—especially farmers—couldn't pay back the banks. Bryan based his campaign around the free silver movement. He said the government should switch from gold to silver because it was more plentiful. That way, more paper money would be in circulation. If there was additional money circulating, the farmers could earn more profits and pay back their loans.

Republican candidate William McKinley defeated Bryan in 1896. Still, Bryan's ideas were not lost. His basic philosophies influenced many important political leaders.

Robert M. La Follette was another Progressive leader with rural roots. He was born in 1855 to a poverty-stricken farming family in Primrose, Wisconsin. After serving three terms in Congress (1885–1891), he lost the election in 1890.

Afterward, La Follette started his own private law practice. While practicing law, he observed "inside" (secret) deals being made between the state's industry leaders and political leaders. La Follette believed that these inside agreements cheated farmers and small businessmen.

What La Follette witnessed motivated him to run for governor of Wisconsin in 1900. His

Robert Marion La Follette (1855–1925) was an attorney who became Wisconsin's governor in 1901, a term he held until 1906. He continued his political career, becoming a senator in 1906 and a presidential nominee in 1924.

platform was a model of Progressive thought. He promoted fair and equal taxation of corporate property, regulation of railroads, and protection of public resources. He won the election for the Republican Party. His push for

MR. LA FOLLETTE'S STRONGEST CARD.

WISCONSIN

BEFORE AND AFTER

THE

"EXHIBIT A"

LAFOLLETTE REFORMS

This 1911 political cartoon exaggerated the strengths of Robert M. La Follette, whose Progressive politics during his term in the U.S. Senate helped regulate the railroad industry. During his term, La Follette announced that the entire United States economy was controlled by key investment groups, namely those run by J. P. Morgan and John D. Rockefeller. La Follette imposed laws that helped break down executive power while empowering America's workers.

laws that gave more power to the people was called the "Wisconsin Idea."

After one term, La Follette ran for the U.S. Senate in 1906 and won again. Throughout his career, he pushed for Progressive laws and challenged conservatives.

The Progressive Party was officially formed in 1912. Twelve years later, La Follette ran as an independent Progressive candidate for president. As a national candidate, he spoke against the control of industry and government by private monopolies. True to his roots, La Follette favored lower taxes for the poor. He insisted that the people should own the country's natural resources and railroads.

Chapter Two

A Square Deal

O ne of the most well-known Progressive leaders was Theodore Roosevelt. He was born in 1858. Unlike previous Progressives, Roosevelt was born and raised in New York City. Because of his urban roots, Roosevelt's ideas about Progressive politics were different.

As a young man, Roosevelt served three terms in the New York State Assembly. As New York's police commissioner, he fought corruption on the police force. Starting in 1897, Roosevelt served for three years as assistant secretary of the navy for Republican president William McKinley.

When McKinley decided to run for a second term, he asked Roosevelt to be his vice presidential running mate. Roosevelt believed this was an insignificant position. He only accepted the nomination under pressure from party leaders.

President Theodore Roosevelt (1858–1919) became the president of the United States in 1901 (after President William McKinley's death by assassination). In this 1903 photograph, Roosevelt gives a speech in Wyoming. Among Roosevelt's most notable accomplishments were the construction of the Panama Canal in 1904 and the ending of the Russo-Japanese War (for which he earned the 1906 Nobel Peace Prize).

Several months after winning the election, McKinley was assassinated. On September 14, 1901, Roosevelt was sworn in as the twenty-sixth president of the United States. At forty-two years old, he was the youngest man to ever become president.

Roosevelt described his political beliefs as the "Square Deal" policy. Under his watch, no one would receive special treatment; everyone would be treated "fair and square." In one speech, Roosevelt said, "The rich man should have justice, and the poor man should have justice, and no man should have more or less."

Roosevelt's first notable act was to take on trusts. Trusts were large corporations that controlled many other

Upton Sinclair

Upton Sinclair was a writer born in Maryland in 1878. He is most well-known for his book *The Jungle*, which showed the horrible working conditions in the meat-packing industry. It was a best-selling book, and Americans were shocked by what they read. After President Theodore Roosevelt read *The Jungle*, he ordered an investigation of the industry. The same year Sinclair's work was published, Congress passed the Pure Food and Drug Act (1906) and the Meat Inspection Act (1906). Sinclair is remembered for being a muckraker because he exposed people to the dangers and poor conditions of American industry.

companies in the same industry. Trusts were known for fixing prices to drive their competition out of business. Price fixing is the illegal agreement between companies regarding the prices of their goods or services. In 1902, Roosevelt shocked the business world when he ordered the breakup of J. P. Morgan's railroad company, Northern Securities. During his presidency, forty-three companies were sued under the Sherman Antitrust Act, a national act passed in 1890. Its purpose was to regulate business practices and limit the formation of monopolies.

In 1902, Roosevelt involved himself in a labor dispute in Pennsylvania. Miners there decided to go on strike. The

This nineteenth-century political cartoon lampoons the outgoing nature of President Roosevelt. Despite his physical limitations (he suffered from asthma), he remained active.

United Mine Workers of America demanded better wages, a shorter workday, and safer working conditions. The owners of the mines, J. P. Morgan and George Baer, were not interested in hearing their complaints. No one was willing to budge an inch.

With winter approaching and fuel in short supply, Roosevelt decided to step in. He created a commission to study working conditions in the mines. He asked both labor leaders and company management to accept the commission's conclusions. If management resisted, Roosevelt said he would seize the mines. Morgan and Baer were furious but gave in. The commission settled the strike in favor of the workers.

Roosevelt's popularity was high, but not everyone agreed with his politics. Republican senator Marcus Hanna openly described him as a "hotheaded cowboy." During his campaign for reelection in 1904, one corporate leader started a "Stop Roosevelt" campaign. But

These people are being evicted from their homes for not paying rent after the Anthracite Mining Strike of 1902. Miners who wanted to work fewer hours for higher wages walked out in June. By July, the strike had become violent. Soon, soldiers were called in to operate the mines. The strike ended with some improvements for miners on October 23, but the United Mine Workers of America was not yet recognized as a union.

Roosevelt's opponents had little effect on his popularity; he won his second term as president by a wide margin.

During his second term, Roosevelt focused on the environment. Over eight years, he set aside 125 million acres (50.5 million hectares) of forest for preservation. He also doubled the number of national parks and established Arizona's Grand Canyon National Park, Colorado's Mesa Verde National Park, and Washington's Olympic National Park.

Chapter Three

The Golden Age

Roosevelt declared at the start of his second term that he would not run for president for a third time. Although he later regretted his statement, he felt it was important to keep his word.

Republican candidate William Howard Taft won Roosevelt's endorsement and the next election. Although Roosevelt supported him at first, over time he began to criticize his former secretary of war and friend. Roosevelt claimed Taft was too conservative and afraid to stand up to Congress. In February 1912, Roosevelt announced that if offered, he would accept the Republican nomination for president after all.

After an ugly battle, Roosevelt lost the Republican nomination to Taft. Although Roosevelt promised to support whoever was nominated, he went back on his word. Instead, he formed the Progressive Party to run against Taft and the Democratic nominee.

During his campaign, Roosevelt compared his strong will to that of a bull moose. The press liked the description, and the Progressive Party was nicknamed the "Bull Moose Party." Roosevelt's campaign focused on "New Nationalism." He wanted the government to take an active role in promoting equal treatment of all citizens. Roosevelt said, "[Government should] represent all the people rather than any one class or section of the people."

Roosevelt's running mate was Progressive Hiram Johnson. At the time, Johnson was the governor of California and was known for his support of Progressive reforms. Leading other states, Johnson passed laws to restrict child labor. He also passed legislature that gave states the power to control railroad companies.

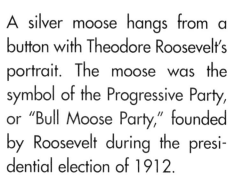

A silver moose hangs from a button with Theodore Roosevelt's portrait. The moose was the symbol of the Progressive Party, or "Bull Moose Party," founded by Roosevelt during the presidential election of 1912.

Eugene V. Debs

Progressive movement leaders didn't always agree on the issues. Some were much more liberal than others. Eugene V. Debs was a political radical and one of President Woodrow Wilson's biggest critics. Debs was an outspoken leader for the labor movement. In the 1912 presidential election, he ran against Wilson as the Socialist Party candidate. In 1918, he was jailed for speaking out against World War I. He again ran for president on the Socialist Party ticket in 1920. Still in prison, he campaigned from his jail cell and received nearly a million votes.

Leading Democrats, including presidential nominee Woodrow Wilson, mocked New Nationalism. Roosevelt lost the election. The Republican vote was split between him and Taft. Democratic nominee Woodrow Wilson won with 42 percent of the vote.

Although Wilson had criticized Roosevelt, he realized that the time had come for many of his Progressive ideas. During Wilson's first two years as president, he promoted and passed a number of reforms.

The Federal Reserve Act (1913) was one of President Wilson's most important accomplishments. This law put banks under the control of the federal government. This national authority decreased the power of the financial

Eugene Victor Debs (1855–1926), a writer, labor activist, and reformer, delivers an anti–World War I speech in this 1918 photograph. Debs led American socialists to form the Socialist Party in the late 1800s and ran as the party's presidential candidate in 1908, 1912, and 1920.

industry. The following year, in 1914, Wilson formed the Federal Trade Commission, which was responsible for enforcing antitrust laws.

To protect workers, Wilson passed the Keating-Owen Child Labor Act in 1916. This law limited the number of hours children could work. The Workingmen's

Compensation Act (1916) provided financial assistance to federal employees injured on the job. The Adamson Act (1916) established an eight-hour workday for railroad employees.

Four constitutional amendments were passed under Wilson's leadership. The Sixteenth Amendment (1913) gave Congress the power to establish a graduated income tax. The Seventeenth Amendment (1913) provided for the election of senators by popular vote. The Eighteenth Amendment (1919) was the Prohibition amendment. It outlawed the making of, sale of, or transportation of alcohol. The Nineteenth Amendment (1920) gave women the right to vote.

Chapter Four

Special Interests

During the Progressive Era, special-interest groups, such as religious organizations and those for minorities, often had a big influence on political leaders. Not all groups were equally successful, however, as there were some changes that U.S. citizens were not ready to embrace.

Throughout the history of the United States, religious leaders have influenced government. During the Progressive Era, the urgency to make the sale of alcohol illegal (Prohibition) started in churches. In 1895, the Anti-Saloon League of America (ASL), whose members were often recruited from Protestant churches, was large enough to hold national conventions.

The ASL began to identify political leaders who favored Prohibition. By 1916, twenty-one states had banned the sale of alcohol in saloons. More and more congressmen

This illustration from 1900 focuses on twelve reasons to abstain from drinking alcohol. The American temperance movement was successful at the turn of the century, and many women led the fight for alcohol reform.

jumped on the Prohibition bandwagon. In 1917, Congress submitted the Eighteenth Amendment to the states. It was passed in 1919. For the most part, the Progressive movement was known for its liberal ideas, but the Eighteenth Amendment showed that the movement had a conservative side, too.

Many Prohibition leaders were women. At that time, only men had the right to vote. When the Eighteenth Amendment was passed, many Prohibition organizers began to fight for women's right to vote. This campaign was called the suffrage movement.

One of the most important suffrage leaders was Carrie Chapman Catt. She was born in Wisconsin in 1859. When she graduated from Iowa State University, she was the only woman in her class.

In 1886, Catt served as a delegate to the National American Woman Suffrage Association (NAWSA). At the

Carrie Chapman Catt (1859–1947), feminist and president of the National American Woman Suffrage Association, took part in this New York parade to promote suffrage rights for women. Catt led the suffrage movement for twenty-five years and was a principal organizer who helped Congress adopt the Nineteenth Amendment to the Constitution, which gave women the same right to vote as men.

time, Susan B. Anthony, a well-known women's activist, was the president of the NAWSA. Anthony had dedicated her entire life to the suffrage movement, but when she stepped down in 1900, Catt took her place.

At times, Catt fought with other influential members of the NAWSA. Some members felt she compromised too much. However, it was her style of leadership—progressive, not radical—that convinced President Wilson to support suffrage. Under his leadership, the Nineteenth Amendment was passed in 1920, and women gained the right to vote. Catt used compromise to push her agenda.

Not all minorities received equal treatment during the Progressive Era. While politicians addressed unique issues

Jim Crow Laws

In the landmark 1896 *Plessy v. Ferguson* decision, the U.S. Supreme Court ruled that segregating people by race was legal. This ruling led many states to pass Jim Crow laws. These laws kept blacks out of many schools, restaurants, and hospitals. Signs that said "Whites Only" or "Colored" were posted at water fountains, waiting rooms, and restrooms. During the Progressive Era, some Jim Crow laws were eliminated, but many remained in place until 1954. At that time, the U.S. Supreme Court reversed its 1896 decision. Although it was illegal, many private businesses continued to segregate their patrons.

that came with an expanding immigrant population, the problems of African Americans were ignored. The Fifteenth Amendment (1870) gave blacks the right to vote, but it didn't give them social equality.

W. E. B. DuBois was an African American writer born in 1868. In 1909, he helped form the National Association for the Advancement of Colored People (NAACP). In 1903, he published the well-known book *The Souls of Black Folk*. During the height of the Progressive movement, black Americans suffered from many forms of discrimination.

Segregation laws—Jim Crow laws—increased more and more after the Civil War. Here, a drinking fountain is designated specifically for African Americans and not for whites *(left)*. The U.S. Supreme Court upheld this "separate but equal" segregation status in the landmark case *Plessy v. Ferguson* (1896). W E. B. DuBois (1868–1963, *right*) was an African American writer and activist who spoke out about issues of racism and race relations. DuBois formed the National Association for the Advancement of Colored People in 1909.

At first, DuBois believed in taking on the problems of racism through the political process. After several years of fighting with little results, DuBois changed his mind. He concluded that change would only come with protest. Many historians believe that the Progressive movement did little to support African Americans.

Chapter Five

A Return to Normalcy

During President Wilson's first term, World War I (1914–1918) started in Europe. Wilson was under pressure from many political leaders to enter the conflict to help the United States' allies England and France. Meanwhile, former president Roosevelt criticized Wilson for backing off.

Americans had mixed feelings about entering the war. At the time, the rest of the world's problems seemed distant. Wilson saw entering the war as a distraction, especially since he had promised to focus his attention on domestic issues.

When Wilson ran for reelection in 1916, one of his campaign slogans was "He kept us out of war." Wilson's Republican opponent was Charles Evans Hughes, who lost by only a narrow margin.

As the war raged on and Germany's victories mounted, Wilson knew it was time to act. In April 1917, he asked

President Woodrow Wilson (1856–1924) addressed Congress on April 2, 1917, asking that it approve his decision to enter World War I against Germany. Wilson hoped to establish a peace organization between nations that would help put a stop to World War I and prevent future wars. Unfortunately, entering the conflict was unavoidable, and American men and women headed off to fight the Germans until they surrendered on November 11, 1918.

Congress to declare war on Germany. Two million U.S. troops were sent overseas to assist the Allies. On November 11, 1918, Germany surrendered.

During the war, Wilson promoted the idea of creating an international organization called the League of

Nations. The purpose of the organization was to preserve peace between countries. Not long after the war ended, he presented the Treaty of Versailles to Congress, which included provisions for forming the League of Nations.

Perhaps Wilson didn't realize it, but the United States was changing. After the war ended, Americans became more conservative. They had experienced much change. During the elections of 1918, Congress changed, too. The balance of power shifted from Democrats to Republicans. When it came time for the Senate to decide the fate of the Treaty of Versailles, it failed by seven votes.

The 1920 election ended the Progressive movement. The Democratic nominee was James M. Cox. His vice president was Franklin D. Roosevelt. (Roosevelt would later be elected the nation's thirty-second president in 1933.) Warren G. Harding was the Republican candidate.

While Cox wanted to continue with Wilson's Progressive policies, Harding promised a "return to normalcy" after World War I. Harding felt that government needed to be more "hands-off" with private businesses. Harding won the election with 61 percent of the vote.

As they had felt before the war, Americans wanted to isolate themselves from the rest of the world. Some leaders began to criticize the Progressive movement. Americans felt less tolerant. During this time, interest began in the racist organization known as the Ku Klux Klan. In 1924, Klan membership reached almost 4.5 million people. Anger toward immigrants was also on the rise. In 1920 and 1921, Congress passed two acts that limited immigration.

President Warren G. Harding (1865–1923), seen here in a presidential campaign poster, became president of the United States in 1920. As a Republican, Harding believed that Wilson had weakened the office of the presidency.

Historians have mixed views about the Progressive movement. Most historians view Progressive accomplishments such as antitrust laws, better labor laws, and women's suffrage as positive achievements. Other historians feel that Progressive leaders gave too much power to the government. Either way, the Progressive Era was an important time in American history that continues to influence our government today.

Glossary

assassination (uh-sa-sih-NAY-shun) The murder of an important person.

Congress (KON-gres) The part of the U.S. government that makes laws and is made up of the House of Representatives and the Senate.

conservative (kun-SER-vuh-tiv) A person who favors a policy of keeping things as they are.

corporation (kor-puh-RAY-shun) A group of people who act together under a legal charter as one company with legal privileges and responsibilities.

Democratic Party (deh-muh-KRA-tik PAR-tee) One of the two major political parties in the United States. The Democratic Party usually favors national- and state-sponsored social programs, higher taxes, and lower defense spending.

depression (dih-PREH-shun) A period during which business activities are slow and people are jobless.

liberal (LIH-bu-rul) Politically, having views that favor reform and the use of government power to make those reforms.

monopoly (muh-NAH-puh-lee) Total control by one company or group over a product or service.

nominate (NAH-mih-nayt) The act of proposing a specific candidate for political office.

platform (PLAT-form) The political beliefs expressed by candidates running for office.

Populist Party (POP-yoo-list PAR-tee) A political party formed during the 1890s that represented the interests of workers and farmers.

Progressive Party (proh-GREH-siv PAR-tee) A former U.S. political party founded by Theodore Roosevelt during the presidential campaign of 1912.

Prohibition (proh-uh-BIH-shun) A period in American history (1920–1933) during which alcohol was illegal.

Republican Party (rih-PUH-blih-ken PAR-tee) One of the two major political parties in the United States. The Republican Party usually favors lower taxes, fewer national- and state-sponsored social programs, and higher defense spending.

segregate (SEH-gruh-gayt) To separate people of different races or classes.

suffrage (SUH-frij) The right of voting.

trust (TRUST) A group of corporations that are combined to control prices and reduce competition in a business or industry.

Web Sites

Due to the changing nature of Internet links, the Rosen Publishing Group, Inc., has developed an online list of Web sites related to the subject of this book. This site is updated regularly. Please use this link to access the list:

http://www.rosenlinks.com/pmnhnt/prle

Primary Source Image List

Page 5: G. H. Van Norman took this 1896 photograph of William Jennings Bryan, housed at the U.S. Library of Congress, Washington, D.C.

Page 5 (inset): This cartoon was published in 1900 and is currently housed at the U.S. Library of Congress, Washington, D.C.

Page 7: This 1906 image of Senator Robert M. La Follette is housed at the Wisconsin Historical Society, Madison, Wisconsin.

Page 8: This political cartoon of La Follette originally appeared in the *Chicago Tribune* on December 29, 1911. It appears here courtesy of the Wisconsin Historical Society.

Page 10: This 1903 photograph by R. Y. Young of President Roosevelt is part of the Corbis collection, New York.

Page 12: President Roosevelt can be seen in this political cartoon, once the cover of *The Verdict*, a magazine from 1899. The image is part of the collection of Art Resource in New York.

Page 13: Coal miners are pictured in this 1902 photograph, originally published in *Anthracite Coal Communities*, 1904. It is in the collection of the New York Public Library.

Page 15: President Roosevelt's portrait is visible on this campaign button from 1912, part of the Corbis collection, New York.

Page 17: This 1918 photograph of Eugene V. Debs is part of the Corbis collection, New York.

Page 20: This illustration, "Family Temperance Pledge," dates from 1900. It is part of the Hulton Archive, New York.

Page 21: In this anonymous photograph, suffragist Carrie Chapman Catt marches in a New York parade. This photograph is part of the Corbis collection, New York.

Page 23 (left): Lee Russell took this image of an African American man in Oklahoma City, Oklahoma, in 1939. The image is housed at the U.S. Library of Congress, Washington, D.C.

Page 23 (right): Cornelius M. Battey took this photograph of W. E. B. DuBois in 1919. The image is housed at the U.S. Library of Congress, Washington, D.C.

Page 25: President Woodrow Wilson delivering a speech to Congress on April 2, 1917. The print is housed at the U.S. Library of Congress, Washington, D.C.

Page 27: This poster featuring President Harding is part of the collection of the Ohio Historical Society.

Index

About the Author

Lois Sakany is a freelance writer living in Brooklyn, New York.